Remembering India

*Commemorating the
50th Anniversary
of India's Independence*

SPONSORED BY PRUDENTIAL CORPORATION PLC

REMEMBERING INDIA

David Goodall

David Goodall

SCORPION CAVENDISH

LONDON

Contents

Sponsor's Preface	*Sir Martin Jacomb*	5	
Foreword	*H.E. Dr L.M. Singhvi*	6	
Introduction	*Sir David Goodall*	9	
Map of Plates		15	
List of Plates		16	

The Paintings — 18

Bibliography — 118

Cheshire Homes India: Trustees — 119

Cheshire Homes in India — 120

© Sir David Goodall 1997

All rights reserved. No part of this publication may be transmitted in any form or by any means, electronic or mechanical, including photocopy, recording, or any storage and retrieval system, without the prior permission in writing of the copyright holder.

First published in Great Britain 1997
Scorpion Cavendish Limited
31 Museum Street
London WC1A 1LH   England

ISBN 1 900269 05 8

Design:
Adrian Knowles and Kathi Huidobro

Printed and bound in Great Britain:
Lawrence-Allen
Weston-super-Mare
Avon

Page 2: *Detail of Sheesh Gumbad*

Sponsor's Preface

Sir Martin Jacomb
Chairman, Prudential Corporation plc

Prudential Corporation is honoured to have been invited to sponsor this beautiful album of watercolours by Sir David Goodall. I warmly welcome the initiative of my good friend, Dr L.M. Singhvi, as Indian High Commissioner in London, to mark the historic 50th Anniversary of Independence in this imaginative and lasting way.

Prudential has long taken pride in its record not only as a strong and growing business but also as a good citizen and a caring company. In Britain, this is exemplified by our support for "Crossroads" and "The Princess Royal Trust for Carers". We are therefore happy that all our profits from sales of "Remembering India" will be donated to support the work of The Leonard Cheshire Foundation's 24 homes for disabled people in India.

Prudential's first non-European operation was started in India in 1923. The next 33 years until nationalisation were a time of growth and partnership for us in India. In 1956 we were the largest foreign life insurer. We have now initiated a long-term partnership with the Industrial Credit and Investment Corporation of India in order to contribute to the Indian economy and people.

"Remembering India" reminds us of the soul and spirit of India, with which all foreign investors should feel a deep sense of affinity. Moreover, as Chairman of the British Council, I am well aware of the vital importance of strengthening cultural and educational links between Britain and India. The publication of this album is a token of the very real friendship between our two peoples.

Martin W. Jacomb

Sir Martin Jacomb   Chairman, Prudential Corporation plc

FOREWORD

His Excellency Dr L.M. Singhvi
High Commissioner for India in the U.K.

A hundred years ago, Mark Twain described India to his western readers in an exotic imagery, evocatively and eloquently as "the land of dreams and romance, the country of a hundred nations and a hundred tongues, a thousand religions and two million gods, cradle of the human race, birthplace of human speech, mother of history, grandmother of legend, great-grandmother of tradition, the land that all men desire to see, and having seen once, even by a glimpse, would not give that for the shows of all the rest of the globe combined."

When my friend, Sir David Goodall remembers India through his paintings, as he does in this collection, he makes his paintings speak to us conversationally, intimately, convincingly, in a friendly and winsome way, without hyperbole.

Sir David has himself chosen fifty-one of his watercolours for this book, fifty for the fifty years of India's Independence which the book celebrates and one, as a good wish and symbolic prayer for the bright future of growth and resurgence for India. The collection makes an exquisite album, a beautiful baedeker of some of the great monuments of India's cultural heritage, a few of them in their pristine beauty and glory and many more in romantic ruins reflecting the ravages of time. Each one of Sir David's watercolours is a splendid celebration of India in the time-honoured tradition of artists such as Sir Charles D'Oyly, Emily Eden and Charlotte Canning. Sir David is, however, the first British High Commissioner in India to have followed that honourable tradition, with great distinction, and to have produced a sizeable corpus of work, of which the present book contains a small but representative selection.

There is a medieval myth perpetuated by Sir Henry Wotton's definition of an ambassador as a gentleman sent to lie abroad for the good of his country. Nothing can be farther from the truth and more alien to what ambassadors are called upon to do in the discharge of their diplomatic functions in the world of today. Having been my country's representative for several years, I should know. Indeed, the old myth has been belied and exploded time and time again by ambassadors around the world who bring to bear on diplomacy their creative gifts and who help to build enduring bridges between the countries they represent and the countries to which they are accredited. Sir David Goodall most certainly belonged to that distinguished class.

Travelling the length and breadth of India, Sir David found time to sketch what caught his eye in the maze of Indian diversities. His judgement is impeccable, and he shows himself the master of his craft. He has a lively sense of India. He drank deep at the wells and fountains of Indian heritage and imbibed the visual wealth which he shares with us in this book, which will, I am sure, be a collector's and connoisseur's delight. I hope it is only the first of many more to come.

There are in this collection some of the choicest vignettes from far-flung regions, some of them frequently sketched and a few rarely so. Each one of them has a story to tell and each story is a meaningful annotation to the history, religions and folklore of India. These fifty-one watercolours, between two covers in an elegant book of a modest size, conjure up in an uncanny way the vast expanse of India and its rainbow heritage. Above all, they are a noble expression of love and understanding for the vibrant quintessence of an ancient and enduring civilisation. I admire them with all my heart and that is why I used my licence of friendship with Sir David to persuade him to let a collection of his Indian watercolours see the light of day, not merely in exhibitions, (many of which I had the honour to open), but in the form of a book which might appropriately be published in celebration of Fifty Years of India's Independence. The reluctant Sir David yielded to my persuasion, but left the responsibility of finding a publisher to me.

I mentioned the idea to my helpful and energetic friend, Nicolas Maclean of Pennycross who took it forward and came up with Scorpion Cavendish as publisher and the Prudential Corporation plc as sponsor. Sir Martin Jacomb, Chairman of Prudential Corporation plc and Chairman of the British Council, is an old friend of India. It is generous of Sir Martin, and it speaks volumes for his breadth of vision that under his chairmanship Prudential has agreed to sponsor the five thousand copies of the book, so as to benefit the 24 Leonard Cheshire Homes in India. Under the directorship of Adrian Knowles, Scorpion Cavendish is a publishing house of great repute, with many books on India's art and heritage to their credit and with exceptional enthusiasm and commitment to Indian culture. I am happy to see the eventual fruition of the seed of an idea I happened to plant and am glad to welcome this heart-warming gift of friendship from Sir David Goodall.

L. M. Singhvi

His Excellency Dr L.M. Singhvi
High Commissioner for India in the U.K.

Introduction

"India is a place that changes you", said an elderly friend who had served in India during the Second World War, on hearing that I was being sent to Delhi as British High Commissioner early in 1987. Although almost every native of these islands has something of India in the ancestral bloodstream – in my case a Surgeon from Ireland in the Honourable East India Company's service, who married Lord Lawrence's youngest sister – neither my wife nor I had ever been there or expected to go. But we had not been in India more than a few weeks before we understood the force of my friend's remark and realised that he was right.

Vastness, both in extent and in numbers of people; diversity – of climate, landscape, language and culture; contrasts – of wealth and poverty, sophistication and simplicity, splendour and squalor, entrepreneurial independence and bureaucratic strangulation: all these jostle in one's head when trying to describe the impact of India on someone encountering it for the first time. And even among the computer-linked, high-rise office blocks of Bombay or Bangalore, there is an awareness of the older India persisting not far below the surface: the layer upon layer of culture and civilisation reaching back into antiquity upon which India's nationhood rests; the deep strain of spirituality on which Mahatma Gandhi drew so powerfully, and in which the Hindu and Christian mystical traditions find a meeting point; the faithful religious observance which coexists with the currently fashionable secular materialism.

No one experiencing all this, even from the privileged and protected position of a British High Commissioner, can retain a narrowly Eurocentric understanding of the world or continue to view reality through purely Western spectacles.

During the four and a half years which we spent in India from 1987 to 1991, great changes took place, both in India and in the outside world. The Berlin Wall came down, the Soviet Union dissolved and the end of the Cold War brought about a seismic shift in the international political landscape. India experienced four Prime Ministers – Rajiv Gandhi, V.P. Singh, Chandra Shekhar and Narasimha Rao – and embarked on a far-reaching programme of economic reform. The country became gradually but perceptibly more prosperous, although communal and caste tensions intensified. Relations between Britain and India significantly improved, to a point at which an Indian Minister could dryly observe that "relations between India and Britain are now normal – which is most unusual". In one way or another I was professionally involved in all these developments. One day, perhaps, I may write something about them. But they are not what I am remembering in this book: nor indeed – absorbing though they were – are they what has left the strongest impression on my memory.

When I think of India now, I think first of the many friends we made there: the generosity of their hospitality, the warmth of their welcome and the quality of their conversation: so many highly articulate people interested, (as most British people are not), in abstract ideas – economic, scientific, political and spiritual – and ready at the drop of a hat to expound them with verve and elegance. I remember all those I came across in every corner of India who work with quiet dedication to alleviate poverty or to help the disadvantaged; and I remember my first visit to the Delhi Cheshire Home for the disabled, at the invitation of its indefatigable benefactor and champion, General Virendra Singh; and my subsequent conversation with Leonard Cheshire himself in the garden of my house in Delhi, which led to my joining The Leonard Cheshire Foundation – and eventually to my becoming its chairman. When the time came to leave the British Diplomatic Service, it was India which brought me into another worldwide family – that of the Cheshire Homes, which today help and support disabled people in fifty different countries, from Britain to South Africa and from the Philippines to Ireland.

In a very special way, however, I remember India in terms of my own particular hobby of drawing or painting in watercolours. The sweep and variety of its landscape, the strength and vitality of its colours, and the dramatic splendour and exuberance of its buildings reflecting so many different cultures, make India a landscape painter's paradise. Fortuitously but not inappropriately, it was a handful of British watercolourists who first gave people in Europe a vision of what India looked like: William Hodges, who arrived in India in 1780, and whose watercolours were popularised as aquatints; Thomas and William Daniell, the uncle and nephew who penetrated to parts of India which no European had visited before; Samuel Davis, who was the first to paint the Himalayas, and who ended up as a Director of the Honourable East India Company.

After them came a succession of officers and officials of the Company, and later of the Crown, for whom the drawing of topographical watercolours was a professional requirement, and a long line of gifted amateurs (and their ladies), for whom it was both a polite accomplishment and an essential recreation. The hobby was practiced at the highest level: Lady Emily Eden, sister to Lord Auckland, and Lady Charlotte Canning, the tragic wife of "Clemency" Canning, were both talented watercolourists. Even more powerfully than the Mogul miniature, the romantic vision of India transmitted to us by the eighteenth and early nineteenth century British watercolourists still colours the way in which we perceive the Indian landscape today; and to walk along the Ghats at Varanasi at sunrise is to be transported back into the world of William Daniell or Edward Lear.

So when I took my sketchbook and watercolours with me on my many official journeys around the country and snatched a few moments from an official programme to sit down and make a sketch, I felt that I was following, however inadequately, an honourable tradition. I felt also that it did no harm to the British High Commissioner's image to be known for this mild eccentricity, more unusual than an addiction to golf and certainly less inimical to wildlife than the viceregal fondness for hunting, shooting and pig-sticking.

And so the armed bodyguard with whom I was invested throughout my time in India got used to taking up firing positions around the straw-hatted figure on the camp stool while I quickly sketched a view that caught my eye; and although they fortunately never had to use their weapons in my defence, their presence undoubtedly helped to keep at a distance the crowd of interested onlookers who, unless firmly discouraged, would have got between me and the view I was trying to draw. Meanwhile my Personal Security Officer, V.P. Sharma, and my driver, Imtiaz Ahmed, who patiently accompanied me on so many of my painting forays, became two of my most sympathetic and discerning critics.

In the intervals of conducting business with the Government of India in Delhi, the British High Commissioner is in the happy position of being able – indeed encouraged – to travel the length and breadth of the country at the Queen's expense;

and in the drawings reproduced in this book almost all the states we visited are represented. (The North-Eastern States were off limits to diplomats at the time, and so to my regret do not figure here).

I call them drawings rather than paintings, because that is essentially what they are. With one or two exceptions, they are pen drawings washed in colour rather than "pure" watercolours. Nor have I any illusions about their quality. They are the work of a self-taught amateur who draws and paints for pleasure, and make no claim to be anything more. But the advantage of watercolour drawing as a hobby is that it enables you to get to know the scenes you portray in a uniquely intimate way. A view you have painted is never forgotten: it is assimilated into your memory in a way which photography cannot match, and becomes part of your experience. Years afterwards, when you look at a picture again, every detail of the circumstances in which it was painted comes back to you: the tranquillity of the scene, the villager who brought you a chair while his wife offered you a cup of tea, the difficulty you had with the shadows under the trees, the vivid reds and yellows of the turbaned Rajputs watching you from a respectful distance.

So my tribute to India in this fiftieth year of her independence is not a book of diplomatic memoirs or political analysis, but a collection of pictures which I hope convey some hint at least of the visual pleasure to be derived from travelling round India, and remind me of how fortunate I was to spend the final years of my diplomatic career in such an amazing and fascinating country.

For making this book possible, I am indebted to my friend Dr L.M. Singhvi, Indian High Commissioner in the United Kingdom, whose idea it was; to the Prudential Corporation plc for sponsoring it, and to Nicolas Maclean of Pennycross, and the publisher, Mr Adrian Knowles, for their encouragement and for all the trouble they have taken with the production. Finally, I must record a tribute to the twenty-four Indian Cheshire Homes across the country – from Dehra Dun to Madras and from Bombay to Calcutta – for the pioneering care and support they provide to disabled people of all ages, races and faiths. India had a special place in Leonard Cheshire's heart; it was here that he came to be married to his wife Sue, now Lady Ryder of Warsaw, and here – in Bombay in 1955 – that he opened the first Cheshire Home outside the United Kingdom. I like to think that he would have found in these pictures some faint reflection of his own deep affection for India and the Indian people.

David Goodall *Ampleforth, 1997*

Map of Plates

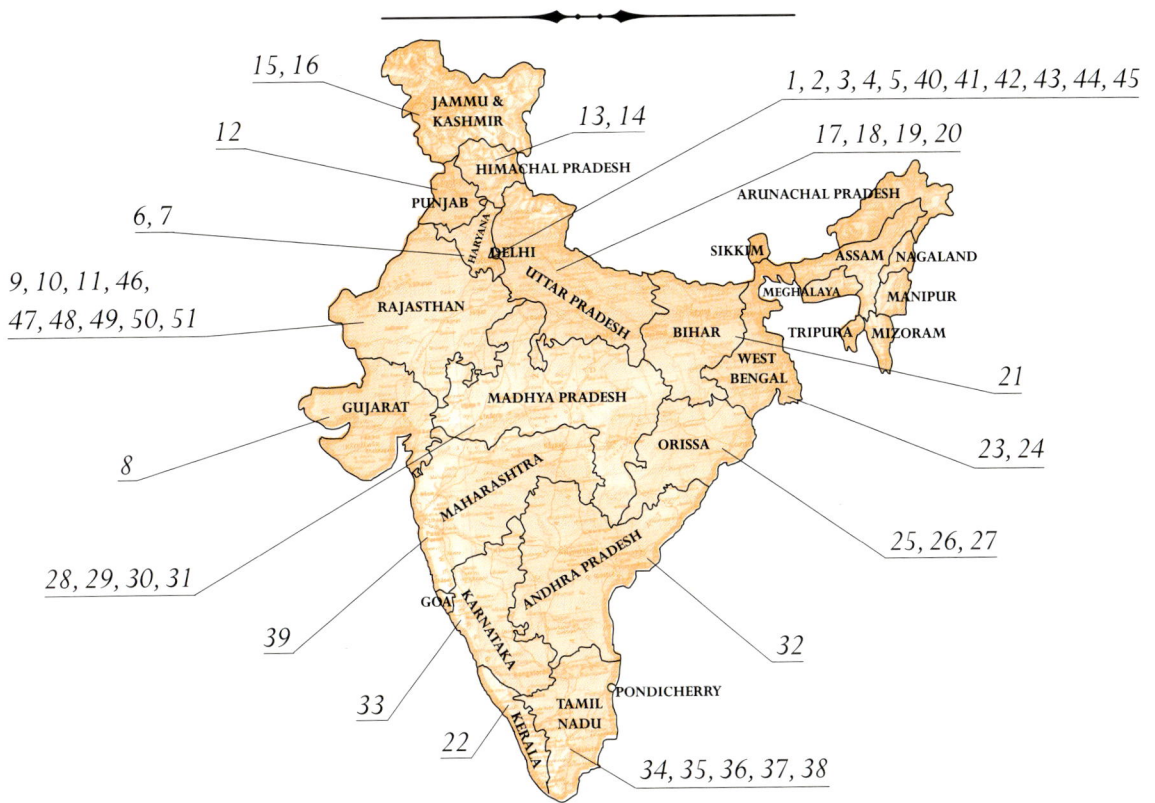

List of Plates

Delhi
		Page
Plate 1	The British High Commissioner's Residence, New Delhi	19
Plate 2	Bara Gumbad	21
Plate 3	Safdarjang's Tomb	23
Plate 4	Sheesh Gumbad	25
Plate 5	The Tomb of Isa Khan	27

Haryana
Plate 6	Part of a Mosque at Bhondsi	29
Plate 7	Tomb at Kurukshetra	29

Gujarat
Plate 8	Jami Masjid, Ahmedabad	31

Rajasthan
Plate 9	Jaisamand	33
Plate 10	Mausoleum at Tijara	35
Plate 11	Kusum Sarovar (Manasi Gangar)	37

Punjab
Plate 12	The Golden Temple, Amritsar	39

Himachal Pradesh
		Page
Plate 13	Paonta Sahib	41
Plate 14	Krishna Temple at Naggar	43

Jammu & Kashmir
Plate 15	Nagin Lake	45
Plate 16	Dal Lake	47

Uttar Pradesh
Plate 17	The British Cemetery at Meerut	49
Plate 18	Basilica at Sardhana	51
Plate 19	The Durga Temple at Varanasi (Benares)	53
Plate 20	Birbal's House, Fatehpur Sikri	55

Bihar
Plate 21	The Tomb of Sher Shah Sur at Sasaram	57

Kerala
Plate 22	Between Kottayam and Aleppey	59

West Bengal
Plate 23	The Victoria Memorial, Calcutta	61
Plate 24	Barrackpore	63

		PAGE
ORISSA		
PLATE 25	The Great Tank at Bhubaneshwar	65
PLATE 26	Rahmeshvara Temple, Bhubaneshwar	67
PLATE 27	The Sun Temple, Konarak	69
MADHYA PRADESH		
PLATE 28	Temple at Khajuraho	71
PLATE 29	Dhubela	73
PLATE 30	Datia	75
PLATE 31	The Midwife's Palace, Mandu	77
ANDHRA PRADESH		
PLATE 32	The Tomb of Hayath Bakshi Begum, Golconda	79
KARNATAKA		
PLATE 33	Mosque at Srirangapatnam	81
TAMIL NADU		
PLATE 34	Kanchipuram	83
PLATE 35	Shore Temple at Mahabalipuram	85
PLATE 36	Tambaram	87
PLATE 37	St Andrew's Kirk, Madras	89
PLATE 38	Kanyakumari	91
MAHARASHTRA		
PLATE 39	Daulatabad	93
DELHI		
PLATE 40	Afsarwala Mosque	95
PLATE 41	Madrasa at Hauz Khas	97
PLATE 42	Begampuri Masjid	99
PLATE 43	Jamali Kamali Mosque	101
PLATE 44	Tombs at Mehrauli	103
PLATE 45	Tomb at Tughluqabad	105
RAJASTHAN		
PLATE 46	Jodhpur Fort	107
PLATE 47	Surya Narayana Temple, Ranakpur	109
PLATE 48	The Lalgarh Palace, Bikaner	111
PLATE 49	Dungar Niwas, Gajner	113
PLATE 50	Chhattri at the Gadisar Tank, Jaisalmer	115
PLATE 51	Neemrana	117

PLATE 1

THE BRITISH HIGH COMMISSIONER'S RESIDENCE, NEW DELHI

The official residence of the British High Commissioner to India is situated away from the so-called "diplomatic ghetto" in Chanakyapuri. So happily the High Commissioner is not obliged to live over the shop. His house is at the end of one of the wide, treelined boulevards with which the ambitious planners of New Delhi wisely endowed the new capital of the Indian Empire – a street now called Rajaji Marg, but formerly King George's Avenue: hence the name "2KG" (2, King George's Avenue), by which it is still known to the High Commissioner and his staff.

Nicknamed "Baker's Oven" in the days before air conditioning, it was designed by Sir Herbert Baker for occupation by a senior government official, and is one of the very few two-storey bungalows, (in India, not a contradiction in terms), included in the original plans for New Delhi. Built in about 1919, it was for some years before the war the home of Sir Shankar Bajpai, an Indian member of the Viceroy's Council.

When India became independent in 1947, with Lord Mountbatten as Governor-General still enjoying the imperial splendours of the Viceroy's House, the British Government judged 2KG to be just about adequate as a temporary residence for its official representatives and leased it from the Indian Government on that basis. Fifty years later, (c'est le provisoire qui dure), it ranks as probably the finest – and almost certainly the most comfortable – of all the ambassadorial residences in the city, (though not by any means the largest). Grand enough for official entertaining, it is still very much a family house and its three acres of garden make it a haven of rest from Delhi's hectic diplomatic life.

Original Size: 28·2 x 21cm

PLATE 2

BARA GUMBAD, DELHI

The imaginatively laid out and well kept Lodi Gardens in the heart of the smartest part of New Delhi are a favourite resort of walkers and joggers, and the middle-aged gentleman you see determinedly puffing his way round the network of paths before breakfast is probably an eminent Secretary to the Government of India or a senior industrialist, seeking to offset the effects of an otherwise sedentary existence.

The Gardens are a beautifully landscaped setting for the profusion of Tombs and Mosques of the Lodi dynasty (1434-1526), from which they take their name. The Bara Gumbad ("great dome"), shown here, is one of the largest and most impressive of these monuments. It comprises an elegantly arcaded prayer hall at right angles to the domed tomb, (from which the graves have vanished). The latter was built in 1484; the prayer hall probably later. This picture has a particular significance for me, because it is the first complete watercolour drawing I made in India, done early in the morning only two days after I presented my Letters of Commission, (as a High Commissioner's credentials are called), to President Zail Singh.

Original Size: 34·4 x 24·3cm

Plate 3

Safdarjang's Tomb, Delhi

Among the Mogul antiquities of Delhi, Safdarjang's Tomb is second in size and splendour only to the Tomb of the Emperor Humayun. Safdarjang himself, however, was a less than glorious figure. Wazir to the Emperor Ahmad Shah in the days when the Mogul empire was disintegrating, he was Nawab of Oudh and a notably unsuccessful general – "one more nail in the coffin of the Mogul Empire", in the words of a current guidebook to Delhi.

Nor has his tomb had a good press. Whereas Humayun's Tomb is acclaimed as a forerunner of the incomparable Taj Mahal, Safdarjang's Tomb, built between 1753 and 1754, is generally seen as a degenerate tailpiece: "the last flicker in the lamp of Mogul architecture", according to the descriptive plaque by the entrance; and Bishop Heber, viewing it in the 1820s, saw it as being "the colour of potted meat".

For all that, the tomb is a magnificent object; and the great walled garden in which it stands is one of the most peaceful places to be found anywhere near the centre of New Delhi, its tranquillity seldom disturbed by more than a handful of discreetly courting couples. I always enjoyed painting there, but I know exactly how Emily Eden felt when trying to sketch Sikandra in 1839, finding it "impossible to make anything of these Mogul buildings, they are all lines and domes, and uncommonly trying to the patience".

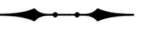

Original Size: 34·1 x 24·3cm

P*late* 4

Sheesh Gumbad, Delhi

Another handsome monument in the Lodi Gardens, adjacent to the Bara Gumbad. Sheesh Gumbad means "glass dome" and it is so called because it was once covered in brilliantly coloured glazed tiles, most of which have now disappeared – although some blue ones still adhere to the main structure. The graves within it are thought to be those of Lodi noblemen who died during the reign of Sikander Lodi (1489-1517).

Original Size: 17 x 20·2cm

PLATE 5

THE TOMB OF ISA KHAN AT DELHI

One of a range of buildings adjacent to the great Tomb of the Emperor Humayun, the tomb of Isa Khan is often missed by visitors because it is hidden within its own semi-ruinous, arcaded enclosure, one side of which is occupied by a disused mosque. Its relative seclusion, the richness of its colouring, (the hard Indian sandstone varying through different shades of rose-red to gold), and the beauty of its proportions make it one of my favourite buildings in Delhi. The first time I painted it, a vulture regarded me quizzically from the broken pinnacle of the dome. After that I drew or painted it at every time of day and in every season, so that my driver would say automatically, when I emerged from the house with pad and painting bag, "Isa Khan, Sahib?"

Built in 1547, it is a particularly fine specimen of the Lodi period; to my eyes at least, more satisfying than the better known Tombs of Muhammad Shah and Sikander Lodi in the Lodi Gardens. Isa Khan Nyazi was an Afghan grandee and commander-in-chief under the Sher Shah Sur, the Afghan Chief who forced the Emperor Humayun into temporary exile.

Original Size: 20·8 x 15cm

PLATE 6

PART OF A MOSQUE AT BHONDSI, HARYANA

Returning home one day in 1987 from an outing to the Damdama reservoir about twenty miles from Delhi, we were passing through the unremarkable village of Bhondsi when I saw the dome of a mosque, surrounded by trees and heavily overgrown with thorn bushes. We stopped to investigate, and this sketch of the crumbling gatehouse was the result. I was told that Bhondsi had been a Moslem village prior to Partition, but was now entirely Hindu, so the mosque had fallen into ruin. Bhondsi subsequently acquired a certain fame as containing the country seat of Mr Chandra Shekhar, the Prime Minister who headed a shortlived minority government from November 1990 to April 1991.

PLATE 7

TOMB AT KURUKSHETRA, HARYANA

Kurukshetra, some 90 miles from Delhi in the direction of Dehra Dun, is a place of Hindu pilgrimage. But in addition to its many Hindu shrines, it contains this exquisite Moslem tomb of Sheikh Chilli Jalal, constructed of creamy white marble and dating from 1585. It incorporates a madrasa, (Islamic college), giving on to an enclosed garden from which, on a very hot, still day in October, on my way back from a visit to the Doon School, I made this drawing.

Original Size: 25·9 x 33·5cm

Original Size: 23·7 x 27cm

PLATE 8

JAMI MASJID, AHMEDABAD, GUJARAT

This great mosque was built by the Sultan Ahmed Shah, the founder of Ahmedabad, in 1424. It incorporates a large quantity of Jain and Hindu masonry, some of which can be seen in this drawing, into its Moslem design.

We visited Ahmedabad in March 1988, when the whole of Western India was afflicted by drought. The hotel we stayed in was described in the guide book as "pleasantly situated overlooking the river". (The River Sabarmati runs through the centre of the city); but no river was to be seen, and the view from our room was across what looked like an enormous desert wadi, desolate, barren and waterless.

I made the mistake of insisting on going to the Jami Masjid on foot. In India, visiting VIPs do not walk. The local police inspector charged with my protection expostulated, then accompanied me wielding his lathi, not just in order to warn passers by to fall back respectfully, but also to deal a resounding blow at each parked car we passed. Out of compassion for the citizenry of Ahmedabad, I made no further attempts at pedestrianism for the rest of my stay.

Jami Masjid
Ahmedabad

Original Size: 22·3 x 15·4cm

PLATE 9

JAISAMAND, RAJASTHAN

This is not the wildlife sanctuary of the same name near Udaipur, but another large man-made lake about 10km from Alwar. We discovered its existence by accident, when my son saw a photograph of it in the Alwar city palace. An immense, lonely stretch of water surrounded by barren ochre-coloured hills, it is bordered by a bund or embankment punctuated with chhattris, (small domed gazebos), ideal places in which to picnic and watch the water birds.

Original Size: 26·7 x 35cm

PLATE 10

MAUSOLEUM AT TIJARA, RAJASTHAN

On the old road from Delhi to Alwar, near the Rajasthan-Haryana border, lies the small village of Tijara. Approaching it by chance one winter afternoon from Alwar, we passed a ruined tomb by the roadside and then saw a little way off the road to our right, on a piece of rising ground fringed by eucalyptus trees, this enormous mausoleum.

Unmentioned in any guide book, semi-ruinous and half surrounded by the vegetable gardens of the village, it towers over an open, undulating fieldscape of maize and sugarcane stretching away to a distant line of hills crowned by a fort. No one in the village could tell us its history, or that of the abandoned mosque which looks over the fields from the other end of the village, except that they were "very old".

With its octagonal plan and familiar domed silhouette, there could be no doubt that the mausoleum was of Lodi origin; but its scale exceeds that of any of the better known tombs of the Lodi period to be found in Delhi. In addition to the mosque, which resembles a smaller version of the mosque of Sher Shah in the Purana Qila, several smaller tombs of the same period can be seen dotted across the surrounding countryside; and it would appear that Tijara was at one time the seat of a Moslem ruler connected with the Lodi dynasty.

The arrival of a Range Rover flying the Union Flag and accompanied by an escort of armed policemen, understandably caused something of a stir; but the local inhabitants appreciated our interest in the ruins, insisted on providing me with a chair, and plied us with bananas and sweet tea while I made my sketch.

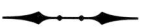

Tijara
15.12.96

Original Size: 21 x 15·6cm

PLATE 11

KUSUM SAROVAR (ALSO KNOWN AS MANASI GANGAR), RAJASTHAN

One of the little known and unexpected delights with which the landscape of Rajasthan is studded, this splendid mausoleum of the great Jat leader Maharaja Suraj Mal of Bharatpur lies in open, semi-desert country between Bharatpur, (now best known for its wonderful bird sanctuary), and Mathura, near the town of Gobhardan, which is a place of Hindu pilgrimage. Suraj Mal died in battle in 1763, and ceiling paintings within the dome of the central pavilion portray some of his triumphs.

A watercolour of the same view painted by Lady Canning in about 1858 shows the Tank and Mausoleum bowered in trees, which have vanished with the deforestation of Rajasthan. Less than half a day's drive from Delhi, Kusum Sarovar today is surprisingly deserted. The crumbling chhattris which fringe the tank make delightful places in which to picnic; but I have never seen another foreign tourist there: it seems to be frequented only by women from the neighbouring villages who come to wash their clothes in the tank.

Kusum Sarovar

4.iv.96

Original Size: 16·4 x 11·8cm

PLATE 12

THE GOLDEN TEMPLE, AMRITSAR, PUNJAB

The holiest shrine of the Sikh religion. The building depicted here is the Harmandir, standing at the centre of the temple complex and in the middle of a great tank, or artificial lake – the Holy Pool. The Harmandir, which houses the sacred scriptures of the Sikhs, the Guru Granth Sahib, was begun in the sixteenth century; but the gilding and marble work date from the nineteenth.

In 1988, I was the first Head of a Western diplomatic mission to be allowed to visit Amritsar, which was still seething with unrest following "Operation Blue Star" – the assault by Indian Security Forces on Sikh separatists in the Temple, which led to Mrs Gandhi's assassination in October 1984. I was taken first to the Jallianwala Bagh, where British troops under General Dyer perpetrated the Amritsar Massacre of 1919 – a poignant moment – but it was not thought safe for me to enter the Golden Temple, which I could only view under heavy police guard from the roof of a neighbouring building. Eighteen months later, my wife and I were welcomed into the Temple by the Temple Manager, Amarjit Singh, and given the opportunity to savour the sense of space, devotion and peace which broods over the whole complex. Standing barefoot and with covered head on the Parikrama – the marble pavement which surrounds the Holy Pool – I was readily given permission to make a sketch, and it is on that sketch that this picture is based.

Original Size: 34·4 x 27·7cm

PLATE 13

PAONTA SAHIB, HIMACHAL PRADESH

Driving from Dehra Dun to Simla, one leaves Uttar Pradesh for Himachal Pradesh on crossing the River Jumna at Paonta Sahib, an important Sikh shrine and place of pilgrimage standing high above the river on the Himachal side. This drawing is based on a sketch taken from the bridge, with the monsoon clouds massing above the Gurudwara.

Paonta Sahib

Original Size: 16.5 x 11.9cm

PLATE 14

KRISHNA TEMPLE AT NAGGAR, HIMACHAL PRADESH

The foothills of the Himalayas are a different world from the rest of India – a world of high mountains, cool, fresh air, rambling stone walls and farmhouses with broad eaves and carved wooden verandahs tucked into the hillsides – ideal walking or trekking country and an escapist's paradise which even the heavy traffic which now rumbles incessantly along the road from Kulu to Manali cannot destroy. A short way off the main road (which runs beside the River Beas) is the picturesque village of Naggar. Its main features are the Castle, which dates from the sixteenth century, and a temple to Vishnu in what is known as the "pagoda" style – a building topped by a succession of pent roofs, each smaller than the one below it.

500 feet and a stiff climb above the village are the fragmentary ruins of the ancient city of Thawa, and among them stands this temple to Krishna the Flute Player. Its exact age is unknown, but it is certainly very old: its curved stone shikhara, characteristic of the Hindu temples of the plains, is a feature thought to have been introduced into the mountains in the seventh or eighth centuries.

I made this drawing under a threat of approaching rain, (which may account for the lopsided appearance of the wooden structure protecting the shikara); and the custodian seen here in front of the building invited us to take shelter and tea in his cottage. It was sparsely furnished, but incongruously contained a large colour television set relaying an international table tennis competition from Tokyo.

Original Size: 21·7 x 23·2cm

PLATE 15

NAGIN LAKE, KASHMIR

During our first summer in India we were lucky enough to be able to spend a week on a houseboat in Kashmir – a holiday which the mounting unrest in the Valley made it impossible to repeat. For security reasons, we arrived by a circuitous inland route from the airport, so my first glimpse of the lake was when I stepped on to the deck of the houseboat and saw this stupendous view in strong, hazy August sunshine: a moment to compare with one's first view of the Taj Mahal at dawn.

Like the Taj Mahal, the legendary beauty of the Valley of Kashmir never disappoints. Even here, however, reality was not far away. As we glided in our shikara, (the Kashmiri equivalent of a gondola), among the waterlilies, watching the kingfishers, there followed immediately behind us another shikara carrying a protective posse of armed policeman. Fortunately they were never called upon to take action. Indeed the only moments during the whole of my time in India when I felt a real need for the protection I was given were when I was attacked by an angry male monkey at Agra and on a visit to the Bombay Stock Exchange, when I was all but submerged in a throng of frantic stock-jobbers.

Original Size: 38 x 29·2cm

PLATE 16

DAL LAKE, KASHMIR

The Dal Lake is the larger of the two lakes adjoining the city of Srinagar and, like the smaller Nagin Lake, famous for its houseboats. I painted this view of it at sunset from the terrace of Pari Mahal, one of the Mogul Gardens for which Kashmir is famous.

An equally spectacular view is to be had from the terrace of the Raj Bhavan – the Governor's Residence – where Nehru, (himself a Kashmiri Brahmin), used to sit in silent contemplation of the beauty below him. When I paid my official call on the Governor, we sat on his verandah where Nehru sat, discussing the troubled state of Kashmiri politics and surveying the immense tranquillity around us, when suddenly a bugler sounded Retreat. All rose silently to attention as the Indian tricolour came slowly down and the profoundly traditional call floated across the Valley.

Original Size: 39·5 x 28·6cm

PLATE 17

THE BRITISH CEMETERY AT MEERUT, UTTAR PRADESH

What is variously known as the First War of Independence, the Sepoy Revolt or (in Britain) the Indian Mutiny broke out on Sunday 10th May 1857 in the military cantonment at Meerut as the officers of the garrison and their wives were getting ready to attend evensong in St. John's Church. The church still stands, well maintained by its congregation of Indian Christians. Neat and classical, with faint echoes of Sir Christopher Wren, it is redolent of the Raj, its rear pews incised to hold the rifles of the British infantry who, after the Mutiny, had to carry their arms with them to church.

A mile or so from the church lies the British cemetery, filled with tombs dating from the early years of the nineteenth century. Originally laid out in an open space, with the tombs ranged along well-kept, symmetrical paths, it is now so overgrown with trees and creeper as to give the impression of a graveyard swallowed up by jungle. In the days of the Company, the British acquired the Indian taste for mausolea, so that now tomb-chests and headstones jostle for position amid the tangled vegetation with massive pyramids, listing columns and crumbling domes. No one with a sense of the past, or alive to "the pleasure of ruins", can fail to be moved by these decaying intimations of human and imperial mortality — even more evocative in this jungle setting than in the restored orderliness of the more famous South Park Street Cemetery in Calcutta.

Original Size: 16·6 x 11·8cm

PLATE 18

BASILICA AT SARDHANA, UTTAR PRADESH

Looking like a piece of Italy dropped down in the middle of the North Indian Plain, the great church at Sardhana, (a small country town near Meerut), is a memorial to the remarkable career of Begum Samru, a nautch girl at the Mogul court who became a magnate in her own right. Born in about 1750, the daughter of a concubine, she was taken in marriage by an Austrian soldier of fortune called Walter Reinhardt, (known as 'Sombre' or Samru), a sinister adventurer who ended his life as governor of Agra under the Emperor Shah Alam.

After Reinhardt's death, the Begum commanded her own private army, twice saving the life of the Emperor. She narrowly escaped being put to death by her own troops, and eventually became a minor potentate under the Company. Along the way she was received into the Catholic Church in 1781 by an Italian Carmelite from Agra, insisted on having her own bishop and built her own cathedral, completed in 1822. In 1986 it was visited by Pope John Paul and designated a Minor Basilica. Inside it is a massive memorial by a pupil of Canova, showing the Begum enthroned above the officers of her court, which is now an object of veneration by local Christians and Hindus alike.

When I first saw Sardhana in 1988 it was still in the care of Italian Capuchins. The priest in charge, Father Lanfranco, was a person of great warmth and enormous enthusiasm – not least for the beauty of the church of which he was the guardian. He carried us off to the Begum's Palace nearby – now a minor seminary – fed us with a magnificent pasta salad and toasted us in home-made wine poured from a cask labelled "Ad Usum Episcopi".

Sardhana 27.3.97

Original Size: 19.8 x 14.5cm

PLATE 19

THE DURGA TEMPLE AT VARANASI (BENARES), UTTAR PRADESH

My two most vivid memories of Varanasi are of breakfast with the Maharaja on the balcony of his riverside palace-fort of Ramnagar, preceded by a leisurely walk along the Ghats at dawn watching the sun rise over the Ganges. Sadly, that unearthly combination of infinite space, hazy colouring and intense religious activity was quite beyond the scope of my amateur brush and pen. So instead I tried to capture the ominous silhouette of the temple of Durga, goddess of destruction. Built in the eighteenth century by a Bengali Maharani, the temple is stained red with ochre and overrun with monkeys. Viewed, (as here), from across a tank of stagnant water, it appears gratifyingly sinister.

The Durga Temple, Benares

Original Size: 30 x 20·3cm

PLATE 20

BIRBAL'S HOUSE, FATEHPUR SIKRI, UTTAR PRADESH

One of the marvels of India, the deserted but immaculately preserved royal city of Fatehpur Sikri near Agra, built by the Emperor Akbar between 1571 and 1585 and abandoned for lack of water in 1600, is too well known to need description. This view is of part of the Harem, known as Bhirbal Bhavan, or Birbal's House. Covered in fine carving, it was compared by Victor Hugo to a large jewellery box. I drew it on a hot, still afternoon in November, having temporarily escaped from the touts who are more persistent at Fatehpur Sikri than almost anywhere else in India. The city stands high above the surrounding plain, which can just be glimpsed between the house and the low building on the right.

Fatehpur Sikri: Birbal's House — 4.xi.92

Original Size: 21.5 x 15.8cm

THE TOMB OF SHER SHAH SUR AT SASARAM, BIHAR

Sher Shah Sur, an Afghan ruler of Bihar, defeated the Mogul Emperor Humayun in 1540 and forced him into an exile which lasted for fifteen years. Sher Shah died in 1545, having built for himself this spectacular tomb, rightly described as "the apotheosis of the octagonal form of mausoleum" inherited from the Lodis. It is an enormous, five-storey structure standing on a platform surrounded by a lake; and the dome rises 46 metres above the level of the water.

Original Size: 16·5 x 11·8cm

PLATE 22

BETWEEN KOTTAYAM AND ALEPPEY, KERALA

In December 1988, through the kindness of the Mathew family, (proprietors of one of Kerala's principal newspapers), we travelled by launch along the "backwater" canal from Kottayam to Aleppey, through a flat, tranquil and uncrowded landscape of alternating palm groves and paddy fields. The launch made two stops: one to clear the propellor of water-hyacinth, which almost blocked the canal for a distance of half a mile, and once to enable a member of the crew to shin up a palm tree and bring down some coconuts. Bird life was in evidence everywhere: we saw pied kingfishers diving, numerous cormorants, egrets, pond-herons and bee-eaters, and two fine brahminy kites, white-headed and russet red in the evening sunshine.

On the way, the Mathews pointed out the little chapel by the waterside where their parents were married and which is now maintained by the family. Kerala is the most Christian of all the Indian states; it also has the highest literacy rate – and was the first state to elect a communist government.

Between Kottayam & Aleppey

Original Size: 19 x 15·5cm

PLATE 23

THE VICTORIA MEMORIAL, CALCUTTA, WEST BENGAL

One of the most imposing – not to say pompous – monuments to the British Raj, the Victoria Memorial is often spoken of as Lord Curzon's answer to the Taj Mahal. The architect was Sir William Emerson, a practitioner of the "Indo-Saracenic" style, (in which he built Muir College at Allahabad), but the inspiration and the vision were entirely Curzon's: "a building stately, monumental and grand. . . where all classes will learn the lessons of history and see revived before their eyes the marvels of the past".

Constituting both a museum of the history of British rule in India and a physical manifestation of gratitude to the Queen Empress, the Memorial still dominates the southern end of the Maidan, undisturbed by successive Marxist governments of West Bengal, and attracting a constant flood of visitors and sightseers. Among its contents is a fine collection of portraits and landscapes going back to the days of Warren Hastings and including a large selection of the ink and wash drawings by Thomas and William Daniell on which their finished oil paintings and engravings were based.

Victoria Memorial
Calcutta

14.12.96

Original Size: 26·3 x 18·9cm

PLATE 24

BARRACKPORE, WEST BENGAL

Fifteen miles up the Hooghly River from Calcutta lies Barrackpore, summer residence of the Viceroys in the days before the capital was transferred from Calcutta to Delhi. The surviving buildings include Government House itself, a classical mansion of 1813, and a number of smaller buildings and monuments including the grave of Lady Canning, all set in what were once well-manicured riverside gardens. A prominent surviving feature of the grounds is one of the largest Banyan trees in India, under which outdoor receptions used to be held. The building shown here is, (I think), Flagstaff House, used by the Viceroy's Private Secretary and later by the Commander-in-Chief. I made this drawing during a picnic lunch on the lawn in front of the house.

From Barrackpore we crossed the river by ferry to the town of Srirampur (Serampore), once a colony of Denmark, where the great Baptist scholar William Carey took refuge from the British authorities in Calcutta, (who objected to dissenting missionaries). There he founded a Baptist college which is still going strong today, training Protestant pastors from all over India. Also at Serampore is an eighteenth century Catholic mission, part of which is now a flourishing Cheshire Home for disabled people staffed by Indian Sisters of Charity.

17. XI. 90
Barrackpore

Original Size: 29·6 x 23·2cm

PLATE 25

THE GREAT TANK AT BHUBANESHWAR, ORISSA

Bhubaneshwar, the capital of Orissa, is another treasure house of marvellous early Hindu temples dating from the eighth century, several of which are situated round the Great Tank, or Bindu Sagar, shown here. The largest is the Lingaraja Temple, which non-Hindus are not permitted to enter; one can however look into it from a wooden observation platform erected for the benefit of Lord Curzon on one of his viceregal visits. The sketch on which this little drawing is based was made very early on a January morning in an atmosphere of roseate stillness.

The Great Tank at Bhubaneshwar

Original Size: 16·5 x 11·8cm

PLATE 26

RAHMESHVARA TEMPLE, BHUBANESHWAR, ORISSA

Another of Bhubaneshwar's many fine Hindu temples, this one dates from the thirteenth century. It is outside the town on the edge of attractive, open country and looks on to a large tank with stepped sides. When we visited it, we found, (as so often in India), small boys playing an improvised game of cricket on the land just behind it. No security threats were visible anywhere in the offing and my Personal Security Officer quickly joined in.

Original Size: 16.4 x 19.3cm

PLATE 27

THE SUN TEMPLE, KONARAK, ORISSA

The greatest of all the Orissan monuments, the Surya Temple, (Temple of the Sun), at Konarak was built in the thirteenth century by the eastern Ganga King Narasimha, possibly as a memorial to his successful campaign against Moslem armies. Although partly ruinous, it is still recognisably in the form of a huge chariot, the massive superstructure resting on a plinth adorned with twelve pairs of enormous carved wheels and drawn by seven equally enormous horses, (not visible in the picture). Like the Jagannatha (Juggernaut) Temple at Puri, a little further to the south, it is within sight of the sea; and in the days of sail the two temples were important landmarks for mariners, being known as the Black Pagoda, (Konarak) and the White Pagoda, (Puri), respectively.

Temple of the Sun
Konarak

16.2.97

Original Size: 16.5 x 11.8cm

PLATE 28

TEMPLE AT KHAJURAHO, MADHYA PRADESH

Even the most fragmentary and idiosyncratic selection of the sights of India would be incomplete without a mention of Khajuraho, famous for its 25 surviving temples of the Chandela dynasty (950 to 1050 AD) and notorious for the exuberantly erotic carvings with which several of them are decorated. I no longer have the three or four watercolours which I painted while we were there, but this sepia drawing of the Vishvanatha Temple may give some faint idea of the scale and intricacy of a typical Khajuraho temple. The temple is dedicated to Siva, and I am told that no less than 602 divinities and surasundaris, (heavenly maidens), can be counted on its various walls.

Original Size: 22 x 28·5cm

PLATE 29

DHUBELA, MADHYA PRADESH

On the way from Khajuraho to Orchha, near the village of Dhubela, my eye was caught by a massive domed structure, half mausoleum and half fortress, backed by bare, purple-pink hills and standing in a semi-desert landscape relieved by a small lake and strewn with Moslem tombs. There was no one on hand to ask for information, nor have I subsequently been able to discover anything about either the buildings or the lake. They simply constitute one of those intriguingly picturesque but unexplained memorials of the past which make the Indian countryside so fascinating to travel through.

Original Size: 24.4 x 18cm

PLATE 30

DATIA, MADHYA PRADESH

Built along the top of a rocky hill by the Bundela Chief Bir Singh Deo in about 1620, the Nrising Dev Palace at Datia, (about 15 miles from Jhansi), is perhaps the most magnificent of all the Indian palace-forts. Sir Edwin Lutyens, who had a notoriously low opinion of Indian architecture in general, thought it "one of the most interesting buildings architecturally in the whole of India", and it provided some of the inspiration for his Viceroy's House at Delhi, now the Rashtrapati Bhavan.

Already more than sixty years abandoned when Lord Curzon held a durbar here in 1902, it stands today intact but totally deserted, a palace of Rajput ghosts crowned by its towering central pavilion, the Govind Mandir. When we visited it on our way to its sister palace at Orchha in the winter of 1989, we had the whole vast structure to ourselves. Climbing through a network of echoing passages and intricate bridges to the top of the Govind Mandir, we surveyed an immense stretch of countryside, while griffin vultures wheeled beneath us, and we conjured up the troubled and bloody history of the Bundela rajas.

This distant impression of the palace aims to capture something of the drama of its ascending array of domed chhattris culminating in the dome of the Govind Mandir.

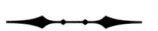

Original Size: 28·8 x 22·1cm

PLATE 31

THE MIDWIFE'S PALACE, MANDU, MADHYA PRADESH

Mandu in central India is the largest hill-fort in the Sub-continent, nearly 40 miles in circumference and enclosing a bewildering and splendid agglomeration of palaces, mosques, tombs and lakes dating from the early fifteenth century. From 1401 to 1526 it was the seat of the Khalji sultans, under whom it was known as the City of Joy. A string of domed stone kiosks links it to the town of Dhar twenty miles away, so ingeniously spaced and constructed that, (it is said), a shout raised in Dhar would carry by a series of echoes to Mandu, and give advance notice of the sultan's return to his capital. It is best to visit it, as we did, during the Monsoon, when the lakes are full and the vegetation at its most luxuriant.

The tomb shown here is the Dai-Ki-Chhoti Bahan-Ka-Mahal, known more manageably as the Midwife's Palace, a majestic domed octagon standing in lush countryside on the edge of a small lake.

Original Size: 16·5 x 11·8cm

PLATE 32

THE TOMB OF HAYATH BAKSHI BEGUM, GOLCONDA, ANDHRA PRADESH

A short distance outside Hyderabad lies the great ruined fort of Golconda; and within sight of the fort is a complex of ornately decorated tombs and mosques comprising the resting places of members of the Qutb Shahi dynasty, which ruled the Deccan from 1518 until it was extinguished by Aurangzeb in 1687. The tomb shown here is that of Hayath Bakshi Begum, daughter of the Sultan Muhammad Qutb Shah, (founder of the city of Hyderabad), who reigned from 1580 to 1612, and wife of his successor. She died in 1618.

Of Turkish origin, the Qutb Shahi sultans adopted a unique architectural style in which Persian, Pathan and Hindu forms are combined to produce a richly decorative effect. The enormous Charminar arch in the centre of Hyderabad, (built in 1581), is another outstanding example.

Tomb of Hayath Baksh Begum
Golconda A.P.

Original Size: 26.4 x 20.1cm

PLATE 33

Mosque at Srirangapatnam, Karnataka

Readers of Wilkie Collins are unlikely to forget the storming of Seringapatam, during which the yellow diamond known as the Moonstone was stolen by a British officer from "the forehead of the four-handed Indian god who typifies the moon". The death of Tipu Sultan and the fall of Seringapatam in 1799 marked the end of the long struggle between the Mysore Rajas and the British, allied to the Nizam of Hyderabad.

Today, traces of the vanquished Tipu Sultan are markedly more in evidence than those of his British conquerors. The domed, octagonal tomb of Colonel Baillie, whom Tipu held prisoner, stands neglected close by the lavishly restored tombs of Hyder Ali and Tipu Sultan himself, who was buried by the British with full military honours. Not far away is this magnificent Jami Mashid, built by Tipu Sultan in 1787 and still in use.

Srirangapatnam

Original Size: 16.5 x 11.8cm

PLATE 34

KANCHIPURAM, TAMIL NADU

Kanchipuram, near Madras, is famous for its temples and for being the seat of one of the four Shankaracharyas, who enjoy a special status as teachers and leaders of Hinduism. When we visited it in July 1987, the gigantic wheeled chariot which carries the image of Jagannatha (Juggernaut) was standing in its central square. At the Circuit House I encountered the first of many local Guards of Honour (complete with bugler) and was ceremonially escorted into the Devarajaswami temple by two drummers and a trumpeter. The street scene shown here has no feature of special interest but simply struck me as being typical of small towns all over India.

Kanchipuram

Original Size: 16.8 x 11.8cm

PLATE 35

SHORE TEMPLE AT MAHABALIPURAM, TAMIL NADU

In the seventh and eighth centuries A.D., Mahabalipuram (or Mamallapuram) was the port for Kanchipuram, seat of the Pallava dynasty, and it contains a justly celebrated collection of monuments of that early period. The most remarkable is the enormous rock-carving known as "Arjuna's Penance"; but in a different way equally striking is this eighth century temple on the sea shore.

Heavily eroded, and with only its two towers standing, the Shore Temple, like Betjeman's Anglo-Irish mausoleum, "sings its own sea-blown Te Deum" to the Bay of Bengal. It is protected by a causeway on which I sat to sketch it, attended by a whole galaxy of helpful officials and policemen, one of whom (to my family's amusement) held a large umbrella over my head to shield me from the sun.

Mahabalipuram

27.X.96

Original Size: 20·3 x 15·3cm

PLATE 36

TAMBARAM, TAMIL NADU

On our first trip to South India my wife and I stayed at the luxurious seaside hotel of Fisherman's Cove, near Mahabalipuram – memorable for me because of an armed soldier posted outside our bedroom who came crashingly to attention and presented arms every time I came out or went in.

Driving from there across country to Madras, we stopped for petrol in a place which I later identified from the map as Tambaram – I hope correctly: as a result of the Indian authorities' preoccupation with security, maps available to tourists bear only a rough approximation to what is to be found on the ground. Unnoticed in most guide books, the place had an immediate charm and has stayed in my memory ever since as being the archetypal small Tamil Nadu township, busy and friendly, centred on its huge tank, with the pantiled white cottages of the bazaar dominated by the gopuram, (gate tower), of its main temple.

Original Size: 21·4 x 16cm

PLATE 37

ST ANDREW'S KIRK, MADRAS, TAMIL NADU

There is at first sight something decidedly exotic about a Scottish Presbyterian Church in the centre of Madras – not least one which looks as if it has strayed from the confines of Edinburgh New Town. But the Scots, like the Irish, served the Company and later the Raj in great numbers; and the splendour of St Andrew's reflects the affluence of the community of administrators and merchants who erected it.

The result is undoubtedly one of the most elegant of all the many churches which the British bequeathed to India. It was built in 1820 to the designs of an officer of the Madras Engineers called Thomas de Havilland, and no expense was spared in its construction or furnishings. Circular in plan, it has a marble floor and a domed ceiling coated with a mixture of crushed seashells and lapis lazuli. Lovingly cared for and in immaculate condition inside, it now belongs to the Church of South India and is still in regular use.

St. Andrew's Kirk
Madras

29.1X.96

Original Size: 15·8 x 20·5 cm

PLATE 38

KANYAKUMARI, TAMIL NADU

Kanyakumari is a small port on Cape Comorin, at the extreme southern tip of India – the point at which the Bay of Bengal meets the Indian Ocean. Its general air is of a cheerfully unsophisticated seaside resort – a kind of South Indian Blackpool. We stood among the candy-floss and souvenir stalls watching a perilously overloaded ferryboat pitching and rolling through the waves as it carried pilgrims to the Vivekananda Memorial, a temple-like structure on a rocky island about half a mile out to sea.

On land, the most prominent feature of the town is neither a temple nor a mosque, but a Christian church, (seen in the centre of the picture). This splendid late nineteenth century Gothic confection dedicated to Our Lady of Good Counsel, colourwashed in cream and appearing to be of beaten gold when the sunlight falls on it, is a reminder that Christianity in India is not just a colonial importation, but was indigenised very early in Kerala and Tamil Nadu, where it is believed to have been brought in the first century by St. Thomas the Apostle.

Kanyakumari

Original Size: 16·5 x 11·8cm

Plate 39

Daulatabad, Maharashtra

On our way back from Ellora to Aurangabad one late afternoon in December 1990, we rounded a corner in the road and came suddenly upon this view of the ruined city of Daulatabad, crowned by its towering hill-fort and silhouetted against a setting sun. It is a monument to the megalomania of Ghias-ud-din Tughluq's successor as Sultan of Delhi, Muhammad bin Tughluq, who conceived the idea of moving the entire population of Delhi to a new capital 1,100km to the south, to a town called Deogiri which he re-named Daulatabad. But the move was not a success, and a few years later they had to be moved back again. The distinctive minaret on the left is the Chand Minar, built in 1435, a tower of victory like the Qutb Minar at Delhi.

I would love to have explored the splendours of Daulatabad more closely, but the timetable was as usual inexorable, and I had to be content with this distant, though dramatic, glimpse.

DAULATABAD

Original Size: 34·5 x 24cm

PLATE 40

AFSARWALA MOSQUE, DELHI

Like the Tomb of Isa Khan, the Afsarwala Mosque is situated in a walled enclosure close to the tomb of the Emperor Humayun; and as with Isa Khan's tomb, the mosque and its enclosure are often overlooked by tourists and therefore surprisingly peaceful. This watercolour shows the mosque during the Monsoon, in a brief interval of sunshine between heavy rainshowers. It dates from the same period as Humayun's Tomb (mid sixteenth century) but no one knows who the Afsar (officer) was who built it.

Original Size: 31 x 25cm

PLATE 41

MADRASA AT HAUZ KHAS, DELHI

The enormous fourteenth century tank and related range of buildings and tombs known as Hauz-Khas in South Delhi are hidden behind what was until recently still a village of narrow lanes and wandering cows. The cows are still there, looking slightly bemused, but the village is now awash with smart little boutiques and art galleries selling clothes, pictures, antiques and artefacts to fashionable Delhiites and foreigners. At the end of the shopping street is the entrance to another world: the tomb and madrasa of Firuz Shah Tughluq (1351-88). On the side, away from this drawing, the buildings overlook a vast expanse of ground stretching away to Green Park to the north and containing the tank which was built to supply water to Siri, the second city of Delhi, built by Ala-ud-din Khalji in about 1303.

This sketch was made on a recent return visit to Delhi, part of the charm of the site lying in its seclusion. No one approached me while I was drawing except the proprietor of the bicycle. Bureaucratically equipped with a millboard and sheaf of forms, and with the diligence of a quartermaster-sergeant on his rounds, he politely but mysteriously asked and noted down my country of origin and other particulars.

Madrasa at Hauz Khas
5.3.97

97

Original Size: 24 x 16.5cm

PLATE 42

BEGAMPURI MASJID, DELHI

Reputedly built in about 1387 by Khan-i-Jahan Junan Shah, Prime Minister to Firuz Shah Tughluq, this large abandoned mosque is named after the village of Begampur, now swallowed up in the urban sprawl of the ever-expanding southern suburbs of Delhi. Despite this, the mosque is a solitary, almost eerie, place. Few tourists ever find it, and its enormous arcaded courtyard has a remote and primitive air. One of the few places in Delhi where one can draw or paint without much fear of interruption by interested bystanders!

Begampuri Masjid

Original Size: 20.7 x 15cm

PLATE 43

JAMALI KAMALI MOSQUE, DELHI

On the outer edge of South Delhi, this handsome and unassuming mosque adjoins the tomb of a Moslem saint and poet who wrote under the nom de plume of Jamali, and whom it commemorates. He was born under the last of the Lodi sultans and died in 1535/6 in the reign of the Mogul Emperor Humayun.

In the background can be seen the Qutb Minar, one of the most famous monuments in India. 283 feet high, it dominates the surrounding, tomb-studded landscape and before the age of skyscrapers was the tallest building in Asia. It was completed around A.D. 1200 by the Tughluq Sultan Iltutmish, probably as a tower of victory.

Jamali Kamali

Original Size: 20.5 x 16cm

Plate 44

Tombs at Mehrauli, Delhi

———◆◆———

Immediately to the south of the Qutb Minar, and bounded on the east by the now suburban village of Mehrauli, lies an expanse of uneven wasteland studded with Moslem tombs of all sizes and states of decay – a landscape of the dead, commemorating dynasties and cultures now one with Nineveh and Tyre. Until recent times, the whole of the area now occupied by South Delhi must have looked like this, with major landmarks such as Humayun's Tomb, Safdarjang's Tomb and the Qutb Minar standing out from a sea of lesser ruins.

Here are two of the many crumbling, unidentified tombs which are to be found close to the Jamali Kamali Mosque. The standing figure is that of my ever-helpful Personal Security Officer, Assistant Inspector VP Sharma. A devotee of the English poets, Mr Sharma ("Sharmaji") accompanied me everywhere and became virtually a member of the family. He also provided the introduction to Hindi which in due course led to my elder son Dominic becoming an indologist and Sanskrit scholar.

Tombs near the Jamali Kamali Mosque, old Delhi 10.1.88

Original Size: 34.5 x 24cm

Plate 45

Tomb at Tughluqabad, Delhi

The ruined fortress-city of Tughluqabad lies on the southern outskirts of Delhi, massively evoking Macaulay's

>". . . lordly Volaterrae,
>"Where scowls the far-famed hold
>"Piled by the hands of giants
>"For godlike kings of old."

Across the road which leads past the walls of the citadel stands the mausoleum of its builder, Sultan Ghias-ud-din Tughluq. He reigned from 1321 to 1325, having allegedly engineered the death of his father, and built this tomb for himself. Originally it stood in the centre of a great reservoir; and it is still approached along the causeway which once connected it to the walled city. Today Tughluqabad is inhabited only by a tribe of red-faced monkeys, who sit on its crumbling walls eyeing human intruders with venomous suspicion, while kites and vultures circle overhead.

Original Size: 32·6 x 22cm

PLATE 46

JODHPUR FORT, RAJASTHAN

So numerous and so splendid are the fortresses of Rajasthan that one quickly runs out of superlatives in describing them. Each one has claims to rank as the greatest of them all, and the fort at Jodhpur, dominating not only the city but the desert countryside for eighty miles around, certainly comes near the top of the list. In this drawing, done on the spot, I hope that the drama and extent of this enormous range of fortifications intermingled with palaces speak for themselves.

On our last visit to Jodhpur we were lucky enough to enjoy the hospitality of the present Maharaja, which included a personally conducted tour of the fort and an al fresco supper in the grounds of his palace to celebrate Diwali against a backcloth of fireworks from all over the city.

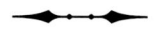

Original Size: 37·7 x 26cm

PLATE 47

SURYA NARAYANA TEMPLE, RANAKPUR, RAJASTHAN

This is one of a notable cluster of Jain Temples built in the fifteenth century on a forest site under the shadow of the great Rajput fortress of Kumbhalgarh near Udaipur. We found our way there up a valley leading from the castle of Ghanerao, where we saw in the New Year of 1988. The central temple, dedicated to Adinath, the Jain revealer of truth, I remember as a complex of interlocking halls and domes, ornately carved and suffused with a pale, roseate light. But this smaller temple, standing on a raised platform surrounded by forest trees and dedicated to the sun, seemed to me to have a distinctive delicacy of form and decoration which I found irresistible.

Original Size: 16·5 x 11·8cm

PLATE 48

THE LALGARH PALACE, BIKANER, RAJASTHAN

One of our happiest experiences of Indian hospitality was as the guests of the late Karni Singh, Maharaja of Bikaner, in this magnificent palace. It was built at the beginning of the century by Sir Swinton Jacob, foremost practitioner of the "Hindu-Saracenic" style, for the Maharaja Ganga Singh, a beneficent ruler who represented India at the Versailles Conference. Jacob's finest work, Lalgarh is a superb evocation of Rajput splendour, and shows that at New Delhi Lutyens did not work out of a self-created tradition. This impressionistic drawing was done on the evening of our arrival, and fails to do justice to the fineness of the carving with which the whole enormous sandstone structure is decorated.

Our host at Bikaner, who sadly died soon after our visit, was Ganga Singh's grandson, a gentleman of the old school and much beloved. He was also an Olympic clay-pigeon shot and a stout defender of the princely order. On our visit to the old city palace, he arranged for us to be greeted as we drove in by a scarlet-coated military band playing "Auld Lang Syne", followed by "The British Grenadiers". After dinner he showed us a jerky newsreel of his grandfather's Golden Jubilee celebrations in 1937, featuring a top-hatted Viceroy (Lord Linlithgow) sharing a howdah with the Maharaja and clutching anxiously at its rail every time the elephant took a rolling stride forward.

Original Size: 34·5 x 23·5cm

PLATE 49

Dungar Niwas, Gajner, Rajasthan

The summer residence of the Maharajas of Bikaner, about 45 minutes' drive into the desert from the city, this is another rose-red palace overlooking a large, tree-girt lake, lavishly furnished in the high Edwardian manner. The room once occupied by Maharaja Ganga Singh was hung with pictures of luscious Indian semi-nudes, while "The Viceroy's Room" had nothing but Greek maidens in the manner of Alma-Tadema. As I made this drawing, sitting under a sun-umbrella on the terrace, we had a rare sighting of an osprey on the lake.

Dungar Nivas

Original Size: 28·7 x 24cm

PLATE 50

CHHATTRI AT THE GADISAR TANK, JAISALMER, RAJASTHAN

Immediately below the walls of the desert city of Jaisalmer is the Gadisar Tank, approached through a handsome gateway allegedly donated by a courtesan who was the lover of one of the Jaisalmer princes. The tank is an artificial lake which was once a main source of water for the city. More recently, the enclosure which partly surrounds it was a meeting place for political malcontents. This decorative chhattri, or gazebo, is a fine example of one of the most distinctive features of Rajput architecture. To draw it, I sat in the shade of the gatehouse, looking across the water to the open desert.

Original Size: 19·3 x 13·6cm

PLATE 51

NEEMRANA, RAJASTHAN

The village of Neemrana lies just within the boundary of Rajasthan, a mile or so off the main road from Delhi to Jaipur. It is notable for a magnificent (but ruinous) step-well and for this spectacular palace-fort, parts of which are said to date from 1464. Having been for many years overlooked and all but forgotten, it has now been sensitively restored and converted into a hotel of exceptional character and charm.

In September 1991, when it was still in process of restoration and had not yet opened as a hotel, a group of Indian friends and diplomatic colleagues took it for a weekend to give the Goodall family our most memorable farewell party ever, making sure that our parting impression of India would be of hospitality and friendship in a setting of romantic splendour.

On the Sunday morning, I walked from the fort into the village below and took my stand on a crumbling wall to try to catch in this quick sketch the genius of the place and the atmosphere of the moment. While I was sitting drawing in the hot, clear morning sunshine, there floated down from one of the open windows of the fort the sound of flutes, as my two sons embarked on a duet by Telemann: a moment of unforgettable serenity on which to close a diplomatic career.

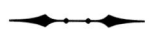

Original Size: 34 x 23.7cm

Bibliography

A complete bibliography would fill several volumes, but here is a short list of, (mainly recent), books which I have found helpful in trying to understand India or which have provided me with inspiration in trying to portray its landscape.

General

Trevor Fishlock: **India File:** John Murray, London, 1983

John Keay: **Into India:** John Murray, London, 1973

V.S.Naipaul: **India: A Million Mutinies Now:** Rupa and Co, Calcutta, 1990

Mark Tully: **No Full Stops in India:** Penguin Books, England, 1993

Bruce Palling: **India: A Literary Companion:** John Murray, London, 1992

Vikram Seth: **A Suitable Boy:** Phoenix House, London, 1993

M.K.Gandhi: **An Autobiography:** Navajivan Publishing House, Ahmedabad (First edition 1927 and 1929)

Portraying the Indian Landscape

Maurice Shellim: **India and the Daniells:** Inchcape, London, 1979

Jagmohan Mahajan: **Picturesque India: Sketches and Travels of Thomas and William Daniell:** Lustre Press Pvt Ltd, India, 1983

Jagmohan Mahajan: **The Raj Landscape:** Spantech Publishers, England, 1988

Viya Dehejia: **Impossible Picturesqueness: Edward Lear's Indian Watercolours 1873-1875:** Mapin Publishing Pvt, Ahmedabad, 1989

Mildred Archer: **British Drawings in the India Office Library:** H.M.S.O., London, 1969

Lord Thorneycroft: **The Amateur: A Companion to Watercolour:** Sidgwick and Jackson, London, 1985 (about watercolours in general, not India.)

Architecture

Christopher Tadgell: **The History of Architecture in India:** Viking, New Delhi, 1990

George Mitchell and Philip Davies: **The Penguin Guide to the Monuments of India** (2 Vols): Penguin Books Ltd, England, 1989

Cheshire Homes India: Trustees

Major-General Virendra Singh (retd) — *Chairman*

Mrs J.S. Aurora

Mr H.P. Bodhanwala

Mr M.A. Chidambaram

Dr W.R. Correa

Major-General K.M. Dhody AVSM (retd) — *Secretary-General, Cheshire Homes India*

Mr K.M. Gherda

Mr P.M. John

Mrs Indira Kothari

Lt-Col P.N. Kak (retd)

General O.P. Malhotra PVSM (retd)

Mr P.S. Maller

Mrs Gita Vishwanathan

Cheshire Homes in India

Bangalore	Jamshedpur	Mumbai (formerly Bombay)
Baroda	Kanpur	Mundiyampakkam
Burnpur	Katpadi	Pune
Chennai (formerly Madras)	Kotra	Ranchi
Coimbatore	Lucknow	Serampore
Coorg (projected)	Madurai	Tollygunge
Dehra Dun	Mangalore	Thiruvananthapuram
Delhi	Mukkampala	Tuticorin

Central Trust Office
c/o Delhi Cheshire Home
Okhla Road
New Delhi 110025

Southern Zone Office
c/o 4, Block 1, RMV IInd Stage
Aswathnagar, Dollar Colony
Bangalore 560 094

THE LEONARD CHESHIRE FOUNDATION
INTERNATIONAL